SPORTS PAGES

Poetry by Arnold Adoff

Birds
Black is brown is tan
friend dog
i am the running girl
Where Wild Willie
The Poetry of Black America:
Anthology of the 20th Century

SPORTS PAGES

by Arnold Adoff

illustrations by Steve Kuzma

A Harper Trophy Book
Harper & Row, Publishers

Sports Pages
Text copyright © 1986 by Arnold Adoff
Illustrations copyright © 1986 by Steven Kuzma
All rights reserved. No part of this book may be
used or reproduced in any manner whatsoever without
written permission except in the case of brief quotations
embodied in critical articles and reviews. Printed in
the United States of America. For information address
Harper & Row Junior Books, 10 East 53rd Street,
New York, N.Y. 10022.

Library of Congress Cataloging-in-Publication Data
Adoff, Arnold.
    Sports pages.

    Summary: Poems about the experiences and feelings
of young athletes involved in various sports.
    1. Sports—Juvenile poetry.   2. Children's poetry,
American.   [1. Sports—Poetry.   2. American poetry]
I. Kuzma, Steve, ill.   II. Title.
PS3551.D66S6 1986   811'.54   85-45169
ISBN 0-397-32102-3
ISBN 0-397-32103-1 (lib. bdg.)

    (A Harper Trophy book)
ISBN 0-06-446098-3 (pbk.)

Published in hardcover by J. B. Lippincott, New York.
First Harper Trophy edition, 1990.

Always for Jaime, Leigh and Title IX

I Move From Sport To Sport.

Alone in my head   during the final heat of the big race,
        or anchored in my place   as our team moves through
those final moments   between a victory   and a sad defeat:
        I move from sport to sport   as the seasons change,
                            as we change
                        and bend and grow.

I   learn.
We learn.   I   know a dream can become reality.
            We know a dream can remain a dream.

Alone   in my head   or taking my place   as part of a team,
        I sweat and worry.   I smile away the nagging fear.
There is always hard work, but near the end of each final
        practice session, I know I am ready to do my final
                            best.
                Win   or   lose   I will do well.

I am getting stronger the longer I play.

I am getting better each day. I can tell.

Alone In The Nets.

I

am

alone   of   course,

in the nets, on this cold and raining afternoon,

and our best defending fullback

is lying on the wet ground   out of position.

Half the opposition is pounding

down the field,

and their lead forward is gliding

so fast, she can just barely keep

the ball in front of her   sliding

foot.

Her cleats are expensive,

and her hair $b_o u_n c_e s$

neatly

like the   after
girls   in the shampoo commercials.

There   is   a   big   grin

on her face.

Now: In This Frozen Moment On This Moving World Through Space

is the right time to ask why am I here just standing

in my frozen place?

Why did I get up on time this morning?

Why did I get up at all?

Why did I listen to the coach and agree to play

this strange position in a r e a l game

in a strange town   on this wet and moving world?

Why is it raining?

Why is it raining so h a r d?

Where

are all of our defenders?

Why do all of our players

do all of the falling

down?

Why am I here?

But Frozen Moments Can Unfreeze And I Can Stretch

and reach for the ball   flying to the corner of

                                        our

                                       goal.

I can reach   and jump
             and dive   into the s p a c e

                 between my out
                     stretched
                       hands

and the outside poles

      of the nets.

My fears evaporate   like my sweat in this chilling

                                breeze,

and I can move with this moving world

and pace my steps

like that   old
          movie

        high
        noon   sheriff in his just

                 right

               time.

That grinning forward gets her shot away too soon,
and I am there, on my own time, in the air,
                              to meet the ball,
and fall on it
for   the save.

I wave my happy ending wave and get up.
                        The game   goes on.

Watch Me On The Wing.

Sweeper: the deeper I can play
              the faster I can lay
out my traps for their fullback
moving too close to mid   field.
I shine along the side   lines
              from mid   field
              back to our goal.

I am the quickest,
        sharpest,
most   intelligent,
(and
most m o d e s t ,) player on
                                                my
                                            team:
        in this league.

I have the

superspeed:

I have the need to do a little

       more

than play only one position. I

defend. I score. I run like

       wind

across the corn fields of

       this

       town.

I am a brown tornado on a

       muddy

       day.

The opposition knows

I come to play with

all I bring. They

       watch:

w a t c h   m e   o n   t h e   w i n g .

Prohibited Acts: Attacking From The Rear. Kicking.   Tripping.

Hitting   or
punching.
Holding.   Pushing.
Roughness.
Using the hands or
arms
intentionally.
Dangerous or wild
play.
Interference.
Blocking with the
shoulder. Kicking
the ball from the
goalie's hands.
Illegally
attacking
the goalie.

Attacking
the
goalie.

Though The Afternoon Was Freezing Cold,

there was a place
in front   of   the
                nets
that was soft and
            dug out.

When the cleats
on my right foot
caught   in that
            soft
                mud,
my body was
already   turning
   and following
   into the play.
My right knee
            was
            turning
                too.

Only my foot
remained
            unmoving
in its   unmoving
                shoe.

This was   definitely   not   a   good   day.

My Knee Is   Only   Sprained,

                 is   only   swollen,
and
the   doctor   says   I   will   be
                              fine.
              I'll play again.

              He says this as he
              sits   on his padded
              leather   chair   that
              can swivel   360 de
                              grees.
Oh
              why can't knees?

Still.   We do not make the Six O'Clock News
              with   this   old   story,   often   told,   of
                       pain and frustration and fear.
Still.
         I must sit on this bench   and be as
still as this brace demands;
         as
still as the other spectators   behind me   in
                                        the stands.
I have been told: next season,
                       next y e ar.

W r e s t l i n g   T h e   B e a s t.

This guy is an animal.   A pig?   Squealing sinus breathing.

A bear?   Hair on his fat arms.

A dog?   No, not biting, but his

c h i n

digging into my collar

bone.

A dragon. Easy. Dragon breath.

An anaconda snake. His mistake:

choke hold around my neck.

A jackal? A hyena? A hungry lion?

A wounded tiger

alone in the dark bush?

A bee?

An

ant? A worm? A toad? A dying fly on the end of a frog's

tongue?

This guy is an animal. A gentle cat rolled

over

by me.

O n e.

T w o.

Three.

23

Coach Says: Listen Sonny, You Are The Safety On This Team,
And Your Body Belongs To Me, And Your Safety Is The Last
Thing On Your Mind. Right? Right. Their Guy Is Super Fast.
Do Not Let Him Get Past. Period. Understood? Safety   Last.
Now Play It By The Numbers.

Simple.

    We start with eleven when the whistle blows,

and

        their quarterback throws his pass.

                Simple.

Number One: He throws the ball.

Number Two: The ball is caught.

Number Three: Their receiver runs

        d o w n   the field

            toward me.

Number Four

Through Ten: My team

        mates   who ought to stop him   are hit

   or

     fall, or miss, or are too slow to make

              the play.

Simple.

    Safety last. I am the last of our eleven,

      and the runner runs my way.

24

Afternoons: One.

The way I am playing this position, I must look like a full back with half a brain. I am too slow. I need a heatrub fix. I am far beyond some green water and a heavily advertised candy bar. Even though I tend to exaggerate during emotional situations, this is the crucial last long moment of this crucial game.

Just when I need that just right word, or clear fact of strategy that might help me get past their monster tackle and lug the ball into the endzone of victory and personal glory, I look toward my bench and blink: I see coach turn his back on me.

Oh

please forgive this bitter moment of mine   as my
face disappears into the mud of the one yard line.

Afternoons: Two.

No one owns
a   foot   ball
on   this
            street.
We roll the
morning
            paper
and
tie   it   with
            old
                rope
and
hope it
            holds
through   the
tough
passing
game.

When you catch my pass   you tuck this paper
in your gut   and make your feet deliver the
                            winning news.

Afternoons: Three.

On the FourthOfJuly

up

on   the   town

hill   there

are

swimming

and

diving

races   and

a

bike rodeo around

the

park.

We have to
run
red markers through
a safety course and
clock our times. We
play catch and sack
                    race
and   learn
                a
        batch of games
where
        no   one   loses
        no   one   wins.
We
pop our wheelies un
                    til
            dark.

Point Guard.

You bring the ball down the court.
The pick is set.
The play is set. The movement of
the ball
is faster
than all
the
d e f e n s i v e
hands and heads,
and you
get free.
You pass into the big girl
at the key. She turns
and
shoots and scores.

The crowd roars.

33

Sweet.

You are at the line. You take a deep breath.
                    You take a deep breath.

You know: a   free   throw
                    is really
        a   free   throw:
                    no hands in your face;
                    no race   down
                                the court;
                    no block,
                    no clock.

This is the place   to score. This is the time to pour   it in,
        and beat those   nasty bad guys   on the   other   team,
                                once   and   for   all.
This is the time to win   this   game.

You bounce the ball once, and wish   for all the luck
                    you know   you   don't need.
You shoot,   and the ball
        flies
                and arcs   and speeds   down   through
                    the hoop   to meet the net.

You get   your point; your score; your wish.   Swish.

Sweet.

My
Short
Story.

I just can't shoot over the shoulders and arms and hands of this monster-with-a-smile who is their center tonight. He swats my shots like so many slow motion flies floating near his head. My dunk is dead. He is too tall. Period.

  He

is a wall of meat in short pants. I just know he must

                                                shave

                                    after every meal:

                                    six times a day.

How can the refs let him play

against my short-legged self?

I feel like some Santa's elf.

My

sweet jump

        shot   hits him in the numbers

                        on his   chest.

                        How do you drive around

                        an 18-wheeling semi for

                        a   lay   up   shot? You

                                                do

                                                not

                                                !

I just can't pass this test

                this

                    game.

I just can't shoot.

I just can't score.

My

short

story is a bore.

Afternoons: Four.

Milkshake with eggs:
my legs up on the
                table
as the screen shows
slow motion secrets
of my favorite pros.
I dream with o p e n
                e y e s
my future d r e a m:
the new K a r e e m.

Even The Light Seems Dark

as it comes in through the dirty windows of the gym.
The afternoon is darkening into evening, and I am
                                 still at work at these machines:
lifting and pulling
t h e s e   weights   until   my shirt is dark   with   sweat.

Then: I get up from the mats and run

    up and down the school stairs: first floor to third,

                  third floor to first,

  over and over and over again.

Then: I do road running and stretching and road running,

  again

until true

    dark and the pale moon begins to r i s e .

Then. Look: no surprise. I am getting stronger,

                am stronger.

                Strong.

  You want to see muscle:

    here is muscle.

  You want to see leg:

    here is leg.

Now I think it's time to bend this toughened knee,

and b e g the coach to let me play on Saturday.

My Team Without Me.

Rough turf,
or an icy surface
                    patch
on   some   strange
                    field,
and I can twist
my ankle   just
           like
           that.
Or a cheap hit
(from my blind
           side,)
can knock
me flat and
                rip
my
        last good knee.

And I will sit on benches
through the longest games
in darkening   afternoons,
that I have ever   had to
      stay seated through,
      and
            only
      see.

44

Exercises: To Be Done Each Day.

1. 30 jumping jacks.

2. 10 windmills.

3. 5 leg crossovers: each leg.

4. 25 leg switches: mountain climbing.

5. 10 hamstring pulls.

6. Trunk rotations.

7. 8 push-ups.

8. 30 sit-ups.

9. Hurdle-stretches.

10. 20 toe-risers.

11. Arm circles.

12. Neck rotations.

Week Before A Monday Meet:

Sunday And Wednesday.   Exercises.

Jog 4 minutes. Run 6 minutes at 1/2 speed.
Walk 2 minutes. Repeat 2 times.
Run 3 minutes at 3/4 speed.
Walk 2 minutes. Repeat 3 times.
Run 60 seconds: hard.
Walk 60 seconds. Repeat 2 times.
Run 5–10 minutes.
Sprint at end.
Jog 6 minutes to cool down.

Monday And Thursday.   Exercises.

Jog 4 minutes: easy.

Run 10 minutes: nonstop. Walk 3 minutes.

Run 60 seconds at 3/4 speed.

Walk 60 seconds.

Repeat 4 times.

Run 5 minutes as hard as you can.

Jog 6 minutes to cool down.

Tuesday And Friday.   Exercises. Jog 5 minutes: easy.

Run 4 minutes at 3/4 speed.

Jog 4 minutes: nonstop. Repeat 3 times.

Run 45 seconds. Walk 60 seconds.

Repeat 4 times.

Run 8 minutes: nonstop. Sprint at end.

Jog 6 minutes to cool down.

Saturday. Warm up. Exercises. Run 20 minutes: nonstop.

Sunday. R e l a x. E a t i c e c r e a m.

YOU

        begin to run
             when
SHE   is almost up
               to
YOU.

YOU   are both moving.
YOU   are staying in
             your
           l a n e .
YOU   are picking up
             speed.

SHE   is stretching
              to
reach your
        retreating
          back,
          and

YOU need
to stretch your
left arm back,
and feel her
smack that baton
into the palm
of your hand,
and
YOU are
off as
fast
as
YOU can sprint.

Afternoons: Five.

On saturday afternoons the downtown community center
gets free   passes to SkateWorld. We spend the d a y
playing   crack the whip   and tag   and bragging   back
                                                      ward
to the heavy metal beat. Our feet flash
                    in mirrored
                          lights.

Mixed Singles.

She tosses the tennis ball   high

into   the   air.

Her

racket comes down harder than I   e v e r

k n e w

a

racket could hit.

It

is a serve into the inside corner,

that I barely see: kicking   chalk

as

it flies away, untouched   by   me

I know this will be love.

Ground

Bound

I

watch:

I hold

my

breath

for

my

bend

ing

friend

on

the

par

all

els.

Even
when I
spot
here
from
this
side I
take
this
balance
r
 i
  d
   e
    .

Dear Horse:

you want this apple.
and I
want that
competition cup.
You
know how to hold your head
up   straight.
I
know how to post so right,
I could hold   a glass
of water in my hand
and not spill a drop.

Please   watch out for pheasants
flying up under your nose. Don't
get thirsty just yet.   Keep
rabbits off
y o u r   toes.

D o n ' t
s t o p.

Last Frame

of
this   game   called
                slow
                pitch:
and
I
whip   that
        ball   sofast,
                even
                under
                hand,

her   bat

is   much

    too

late

    to meet   my

        throw

across   the   plate.

Third strike.

Third o u t .

I

love that l a s t

      great

      shout.

Last   frame.

End of   game.

There Is A Very Ugly

bruise

on the right

       side   of   my

       right

       knee;

and

an o ther very ug
                        ug
                        ugly

bruise

on the right

       side   of   my

       right

       arm;

but the

       charm bracelet on my wrist shines new

       and sweet   as I sip my soda and smile

       into a certain pair of BigBrown eyes

                this friday afternoon.

What a great time to be a g i r l .

These Knees:

these   joints: these soft and floating combinations
                of cartilage and ligament and bone:
these   knees
                were
                made   to bend and flex and
                                        run
                the power of thigh and
                                l e g
                                        muscles
                                together,
        at the instant
        of the   starting
                        gun.

These knees were never made to be hit by shoulder pads,
                or helmets, or the f l y
                                i n g   bodies   of
                                        young   heroes,
                                and   heroines:
                impressing   home
                                town
                                        fans.

63

Equal Curses On Two Long Lines Of Equally Short Ancestors.

Because I am so short, I will crouch down at the plate

and

bend my knees, and try to fool the umpire,

to fool the pitcher

into pitching pitches

outside,

so I can get on base.

Equal curses on that giant of a pitcher,

and his own long lines of ancestors.

Because I am so short, I hate to swing that bat and miss.

I hate to strike out and listen

to my team

mates groan and

shout.

I want to run and hide.

If the ball comes close inside, I won't jump
away.
I stay within
my crouch,
even
if it hits my
knee.

Equal curses on ancestors and pitchers
and pitches   and
on
me.

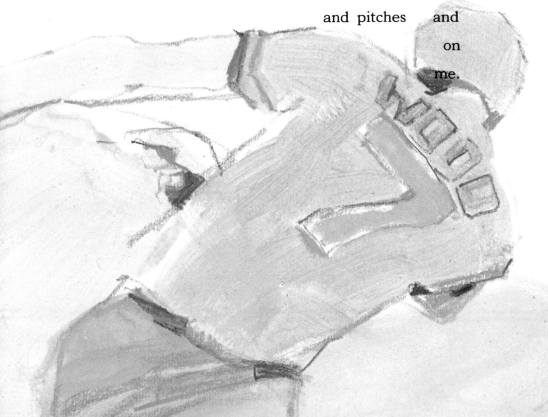
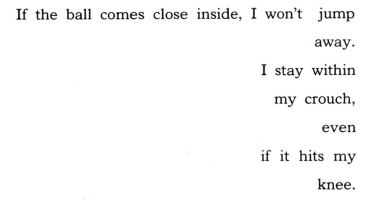

One Finger   Along The Seam Of The Ball,

or
one finger   across the   seam   of the   ball.   Either way
                                                                you
            will be throwing fast balls.
                                    Strikes:
time after time.

Remember: it is in the speed,
                    or
                in taking   a
                            little
                off
                the speed.

Throw   straight.   Don't aim.   Try and throw the   same
                                                                way
                            time after time.

Think of the flapping of wings   through the air,
            or things with fins
                                    moving through   water
            the way the   ball moves through   air.

We always need the wins but your   elbow

is much too

young

for the   curve.

Catcher.

I am always heavy. This mask is pulling down my head. This chest protector feels like some kind of concrete ball deflector.

These shin guards slow my running
Toward first with the faked throw.   I am always late to
                                                    the back stop,
                                            to chase foul balls
                                                    for easy outs.

All my movements   are short and heavy   behind the plate.
I am the battery mate   for the pitcher. I signal the
                                pitcher. I signal the
                                pitch;   signal
                                        w h i c h

infielder will move behind
                        second
            for the pick o f f
                        play.

I am always heavy
in my heavy crouch. But when that slick runner comes on
in from third, and I have the ball   in my mitt, waiting
for his heavy hit,
I am the catcher: rooted to the ground for all it takes.
I hold on to the ball and make the out.

Being   heavy   is what it's all   about.

My Left Foot Is Always   Near The Bag.

First base. I am ready with my glove
    to field grounders, or

                hard

                hit

                line drives.
I am ready
to take the throw and

                step

                on

                first

                base

to   get   the   runner   o u t.

I am ready to put the

                tag

on

an ankle or foot or toe,

and hold on to the ball

and not let go   until

            the

            umpire's

                shout.

My left foot is always   near the bag.

I Am The Best Second
          Base Person

                              on this team, but I play short
                                                          stop,
                              because my arm   is better than
                              any
                              of our   other player's   best.
                              You know
                                            the
                                            other
                              teams have put it to the test.

I can burn my throws straight to first,
and light up the hand
                              inside that first
                                            base
                                            man's
                                            glove.
I love it   when the guy yells:
                              OW!
          G O O D   T H R O W !

I know
   that
   loud
respect.

Sometimes   In Center Field   On A Hot Summer Evening,

when the air is so still   you almost think you hear
                        the mosquitos warming up their engines,
and
our pitcher is getting
the o p p o s i t i o n
to dribble grounders
            to the infield.

              . .

Sometimes   in center field
I have a hard time staying
                        awake.
I never
   close my eyes and fall asleep standing,
                  but my mind will m o v e
                                    o v e r
to last week's extra-inning loss
and my wild toss to third to
                  help
them score and help *us* lose that g a m e.

My throat is always too dry
and there is always an ice
                        cold
                        can
of pop waiting at the   cold
                        pop
                        stand.

One time   a well-hit ball   popped into my outstretched hand
                before I could remember   my name.

Two

Out   In The Bottom Of The Ninth,

and   this   is   the   s l o w m o t i o n   part   of   the   movie.
I
am   in   the   movie,   near   the   end   of   a   long   game.
the   announcer   is   calling   my   name.   The   fans   are   calling
                              my   name.   The   ball   is   flying
                        s l o w l y   over   my   head   as
I   run   s   l   o   w   l   y
            u   n   d   e   r   it: catch   up   with   it   at   the   far   fence.

In   this   moment   of   s l o w   suspense   no   one   knows   how   it
                              will   all   come   out.
The   announcer   and   the   fans   and
                              the
      coach   all   wait.
      The   hitter   waits.
                  I   wait   too.
But
my   feet   have   left   the   ground   and   my   arm   is   stretching
                        higher   than   the   flying   ball.

Then it is all over, and the movie moves ahead: the

ball

is in my glove, and I am s i t t i n g on

the out

field

green.

The game is over, and I imagine   my name

heads the credits spread across s o m e

imaginary

s c r e e n .

We   Have   Our   Moments.

Sometimes   we leap and land.
Sometimes   we trip and fall.
Sometimes   we catch the other team   before they score.
Sometimes   we jump too soon   and get faked out of our
socks.

We can be sharp on the pick-off play at third.
Or
we can have rocks in our heads and miss that
softly batted ball,
and miss that
one
sweet chance to
save
the
day.

I lose. I win. We lose. We win.
The team   finishes   in last place.
The team is
in the play-offs at last
and past defeats f a d e
fast.

We   have   our   moments.   79

Arnold Adoff is the winner of the 1988 National Council of Teachers of English Award for Excellence in Poetry for Children. He was born and educated in New York City, and was a teacher there for twelve years. Mr. Adoff is the distinguished editor of nine anthologies of American poetry and prose, including I AM THE DARKER BROTHER and THE POETRY OF BLACK AMERICA. He is the author of fifteen award-winning collections of poetry for young readers including BLACK IS BROWN IS TAN, EATS: POEMS, and I AM THE RUNNING GIRL. He is the husband of noted author Virginia Hamilton; and their two children, Leigh Hamilton and Jaime Levi, provided much of the inspiration for these sports poems. Mr. Adoff travels widely, working with young authors and their adult friends.

Steve Kuzma enjoys many sports, and his favorites are soccer and skiing. As an active participator in these sports, he is especially sensitive to athletes' emotions during training and competition. He sees sports as an all-important part of the development of mind, body, and spirit together. He is a graduate of Parsons School of Design. His work has appeared in *The New York Times* and on CBS, SIN Television promoting the '85 World Cup, and ABC's coverage of the 1984 Winter Olympics in Sarajevo and the 1984 Summer Olympics in Los Angeles.